limited vision

C. J. Wilson

NEW DAW PUBLISHING
Pasadena, California 91102

Cover by Carlos King and Launi Wilson
Book Design by Launi Wilson

LIMITED VISION

Published by New Dawn Publishing
Pasadena, CA 91102

Library of Congress Cataloging-in Publication Data
Wilson, C.J. (Christy Joy) 1981
Limited Vision/Christy Joy Wilson
p.cm
ISBN 0-9621408-1-3
1. Poetry 2. Literature 3. Wilson, C.J. (Christy Joy)
4. Wilson, Christy (1981)
II. Title

Printed in the United States

First Edition

I dedicate this book and my life to my family

Acknowledgements

I am plugged into the source that gives me the ability to convey this message to teenagers. That source is God.

It was Launi, my sister, who proposed I compile my works into a book when I asked her for a suggestion on how to raise money for my education. In addition, she went the extra mile by designing the book. I will be forever grateful.

I would also like to thank my father and mother for nurturing the gift within me. My works are an example of the knowledge instilled in my heart, soul and mind.

It is with much appreciation that I thank those who helped to underwrite this project; John and Vicki Andrews, Clifford Ashe, Gene and Shirley Browning, Billy and Marilyn Davis, Jr., Tracey Hampton, Michelle McKinney-Hammond, Lisa Hoggs, Dr. Gerald and Germaine Hoke, Derek and Nancy Lewis, Terri McFaddin, Dr. Vena Ricketts, Mitchell Stein.

Contents

from the author:

I can't go to college. My parents can afford my higher education, I have a respectable grade point average and long to attend but I will not go, at least, not with their money.

I Believe Generation "X", does not stand for the *unknown* but Generation "X" *the excellent.* It's now clear my limited vision caused me to know that in theory only. I realized college was coming. I was also aware of its cost for four years to attend a good university. I knew there were full four year scholarships available but I had phone calls to make, new hair styles to fix and the desire to win the coveted "best dressed" award at my school.

Now I can't go to college unless I pay for it. Not because I have to, but because I want to. I started thinking about what my parents could do with my educational fund. Perhaps invest in their retirement or income property, maybe include a vacation they so desperately need or better educate my seven year old sister. They shouldn't have to use it on me. I could have received a scholarship. A little more effort and all would have been paid.

Now my eyes are open. I've decided to take responsibility for my life and use my God-given talent to generate funds for my higher education. Just by buying this book you are investing in my future.

Welcome to my world. Enjoy my works.

C. J. Wilson

hope...

four seasons four characteristics

Rays of light illuminate the sky
as the powder white clouds rest their
heads against its face.
Spring approaches sweetly,
raising curiosity amongst the flowers
causing them to reveal their hiding place.
Small, green, prickly plants burst through the soil
and evolve into lush beds of grass.
Your heart is contented and filled with rivers of bliss.
Pastel smiles and glittering eyes inhabit the countenance.
Love is in the air.
Enchantment, pure felicitation.
Slowly the vernal season fades and turns to summer.
Bubbles of excitement fill the soul.
Outpourings of laughter flood the streets
and joy encumbers your surroundings.
Lazy attitudes and long days consisting of free time.
Replenishing; cleansing.

(cont.)

Before you're given notice,
fall sets in and you become temperamental.
Beautiful autumn leaves are decorated
with intricate detailing and exquisite colors.
The rains arrive and the fireplace becomes familiar.
Thoughts surge through your mind and you begin to change. Preparing
for the next season;
developing, evolving.
The mountains, capped with snow crushed like velvet,
peak and spark your attention.
Lakes glaze over with sheets of crystallized water
reflecting the scenery.
Ice will not live only on the roof
but winter takes a toll on the spirit of a being.
Oftentimes you are snowed in.
You fall on your knees and pray in this rough period
looking ahead to the Spring.

Reflection

Things fall apart.
Nature gives it permission.
However, being able to pick up those things
and begin again is something nature cannot prevent.

facts of life...

high$_{\text{school}}$

❧Boys can be cruel if you don't like their rules
however your years could be destroyed
if their games you don't avoid.

❧ Your first year of high school is not a joke.
You believe institutions of higher education
don't review your transcript in it's entirety?
Think again. This is not a quip, its real life.

❧ Have you ever noticed those who are serious
about their education are also those who are cautious
of the company they keep? Take notes.
You are who you hang around.
Either you're rubbing off on them
or they're changing you.

❧ Read your proverbs. You'll find much of
today's happenings
can be mended by the knowledge they grant.

❧ Your self-esteem determines what you can acquire.
Remember no one can judge you unless you allow it.
The true arbiter is you.

❧ Establish your beliefs. "One who stands for nothing,
falls for everything."

Most importantly, believe in yourself.
If you don't, no one will.

shattered heart...

untitled

Mind boggled, perplexed and awed by your character.
You confuse me yet you elate me, leaving my mind
baffled with scattered thoughts of thee.

Does the mirror wear two faces?
Do you puzzle me purposely?
For I am bewildered and enraptured
by the scent of your cologne and
the perfect facade you present.

I could be mistaken but is that
my heart you're holding?
I am ashamed because I have been
deceived by my own soul.

You betrayed me heart. You cheated soul.
You could not see the lies in the truth
and you did not see the insidious curl of his smile.

You dashed one's hopes.
You failed.
You lose.
And now I cry.

silent tears

Can you hear it?
Can you hear them falling?
Desperately, repeatedly, continuously they are calling.
Trying to force through this disregarded blister,
you can hear it faintly, ill defined, like a whisper.
The facade is so conspicuous,
the mirage like a blunt remark,
voicing, clearly but softly, please let me out of this dark.
Kept in this hiding place of obscure fears,
here is where I am found lying, drowned in silent tears.

Reflection

Once you love, disappointment inevitably follows.
Yet, you always thirst for love once more

friendship...

oneface

Friendship is a term often times used too loosely.
A bond never to be broken.
An envelope never to be sealed.
On one accord;
Tears merge together as your hearts become one.
You breathe in sync,
you love alike.
receptive to compassion...
closed for departure
One face.

Reflection

Sometimes friends are like bubbles;
A little wind blown against them
and they dissolve quickly into thin air.

love..

ode to shakespeare

To him whose love is lost in phrase:
lend thy ear unto me.
The words you've fashioned have
stolen the souls of women
and the men whose eyes look upon them
fill their hearts with contempt.
You say love cannot be altered while many beg to differ.
What love so pure and giving
claimed victory over your heart?
Were your thoughts spoken in vain? Can one find gratification in your
labyrinth of passion?
Please, indulge me.

love has two faces

As thoughts continue to disseminate to an outer limit,
many secrets are unveiled and enigmas solved.
Yet one question remains a conundrum;
can one become acquainted with
another's feeling once more?

This continues to be a riddle beyond my knowledge
lacking the simplicity the heart fervently yearns for.

Love. Complicated in all of its seriousness.
Divine and a true deliverer of heartache.
Love. The lifter of our souls
is also the bearer of bad news and
conveyor of depression.
Its personality is split and its purpose is arcane
until revealed by its other self.

Reflection

Love does not lose, you forfeit.
And the pain that erodes comes not from the loss
but from the bitterness that detains you from
loving again.

disappointment...

general definitions of sadness

Deception.
The principle character in separation.
Division between the heart and the soul;
later, detachment from the mind.
Apart, each give birth to their own passion.
The heart; despair. The soul; anger. The mind; hatred.
If one is not careful, these emotions will erupt,
ignite, and cause you to shut down.

Betrayal.
The most corrupt, yet common form of dishonesty.
It provokes one to seize and destroy all memories
that could possibly give rise to
the revelation of concealed despondency.
As the sole proprietor of festering anger,
its results are detrimental.

Disappointment.
Lover of frustration. The reason why we cry. The excuse we
use when we don't want to say we're hurt. Our friend.

Life is a pain.

the rose withers

Did you ever notice the rose eventually dries up?
Immaculate is its beauty and extraordinary is the smell;
however, the petals soon wither
and the only segment remaining
is the stem retaining the thorns.
Very similar are our envious friends.
Seemingly beautiful in their personality and lovely is
the flow of the fluidity in their speech.
However when our eyes are unveiled
we realize the person we adored was a barbed stalk
ever pricking at the tips of our fingers.
In our garden trust is then uprooted
and replaced by doubt.
Difficult to believe again.

find

Uncertainty
has taken a toll on my heart.

Anxiety
is playing tricks on my soul.

Bitterness
continues to augment in my mind.

And sorrow
is expressed through my face.

No longer will I isolate my feelings
nor will I censor my tears.
My emotions ignite causing a mental break down.
I'm dying, I'm crying,
I'm trying to find you, find love,

Find...

Reflections

Oftentimes words are better left unspoken.
If you step outside of yourself and examine the situation,
you will find that the message is conveyed without them.

family...

guardian angel

An ever flowing river.
Still waters run deep.
Nourishing the roots of my spirit.
My refuge and sanctuary
when the tides rise too high.
Protector of my heart,
believer in my dreams.
Encouraging me to contend.
To keep on truckin'.
He is my daddy.
I am his love child.

sisters

The ties that bind.

My Sisters.

Each possessing innate qualities
which make them equally unique.

My Best Friends.

True to themselves and therefore
genuine in regard to my feelings.
Never forsaking each other.

My Heart.

They are the contents.

it was she

Arguments rang out in the heavens
deliberating her description.
Obviously the conclusion reached
was to let one be pristine.
It was she; immaculate from the inside out
and exemplary from every aspect in my eyes.
A figure to be recognized, loved.
It was she who kissed my fears away
and nurtured the dream I held.
The same person who believed in me
is the reason I refuse to fail.
She is a living witness to the trials and tests of time
but never have I seen her discouraged
nor give up on God.
She lives her life in earnest,
instilling those same characteristics in me.
I am ever thankful for the woman she has become;

Mom.

little sister

The only thing worse than a broken heart
is washing dishes.
And the only thing worse than washing dishes
is having a little sister
who knows more than you.

broken promises...

c'est la vie

You can't choose who will love you
only whose love you will accept.
C'est la vie. Such is life.
Things yearned for by most
bring the greatest strife.
Your goals drift on the horizon,
your dreams washed ashore.
Your love is taken for granted,
you are mistreated once more.
C'est la vie. Such is life.
Small incisions by a knife.
The piercings cause much pain,
the torture never the same.
By stress you are overwhelmed,
your spirit in another realm.
C'est la vie. Such is life.
Please save me from this life.

soul

I've been cut;
a deep gash of relentless agony.
Entrusted was my soul to you
which was forgotten.
Love alters not when two minds concede,
apparently in this attachment the true lover was me.
Yet, the tables will revolve,
forcing you to the very edge.
Grasping feverishly for the survival of the heart inside your head. Dark
forces of nature cloud your spirit
with fears of tormenting pain.
You find as a result of this mishap,
you will never inflict pain purposely again.

your selfish soul

Time is running out, and I stand motionless.
The clock lies illuminated as I race its apathetic hands.
You are impervious to my cries
and your thoughtless words are tearing me apart.
You're so perfect in your own eyes
and oblivious to my pain.
You speak softly to her
as your words propel daggers into my heart.
Your eyes look upon her face
with such compassion and regard
yet with those same instruments you glare vehemently
into my soul imparting fragments of dismal quality.
You incriminate yourself each time you speak,
spewing lies you believe to be true.
However, I don't have to worry
because I know God will deal with you.

God...

The clouds float too low.
Loitering about your head
and causing mental catastrophes.
You then search for something outside of yourself.
Inspirational.

The entity you know and believe
to be the supreme dynamism.
Releasing you from all pressures and life's toils.
Free to explore the sector of your mind
you once restricted.
Not voluntarily but sub-consciously.
Deep down, you possess a life
with unfathomable intrigue.
Unleashed it will be, when you discover that being. Inspirational.

God.

pieces of me

Pieces of me had disappeared
and I knew not where to search.
It was then I realized they had not vanished
but found comfort in someone else.
To retrieve those fragments of myself,
I knew I must delve deeply into my heart
and replenish my soul.
I fell onto my knees and humbly
began to speak to Him in whom I confide.
My thoughts surged from within while tears,
raging, streamed down my face.
I asked for counsel and waited in anticipation.
He heard my prayer.
He answered.
I obeyed.

future...

key to happiness

It belongs to you.
The entirety of this world is yours
if you can live in it.
The treasures you possess are, to others,
sealed and only in the Book of Life are
those treasures revealed.
Rare is the stone from which you were bred,
but beware because in the Bible it said,
“Wrath is cruel and jealousy is outrageous
but who is able to stand against envy?”
Think not of what is received
but of what you are perceived to be.
My greatest discovery,
wisdom is the key to happiness.

metamorphosis

The river trickles along covering each rock,
causing streams to run in directions
which have no destination.
As I walk beside this body of water,
I realize I am being swept into this entity.
My head surges under, hands
struggling to grip the surface
which I fear may be an illusion.
Eventually I emerge and find my past surroundings
transformed and the river has now become an ocean.

Why does this road inevitably disappear?
A perilous journey, must I adhere?
Looking back is harder than proceeding ahead,
For I may not continue and give up instead.
Almost alone, choices become mine,
Attempting to walk this dotted line.
The journey seems so great,
there are battles to be won,
Therefore I shall work in this field,
my back beamed upon by the Son.